LITTLE SOUL AND THE SELVES

Also By Leslie Ullman

Natural Histories

Dreams by No One's Daughter

Slow Work Through Sand

Progress on the Subject of Immensity

Library of Small Happiness

The You That All Along Has Housed You

LITTLE SOUL AND THE SELVES

POEMS BY LESLIE ULLMAN

THREE: A TAOS PRESS

First U.S. edition 2023

Book Design & Typesetting: Lesley Cox, FEEL Design Associates, Taos, NM
Press Logo Design: William Watson, Castro Watson, New York, NY
Front Cover Artwork: *Art Quilt*, Dottie Moore, Rock Hill, SC
Author Photograph: Jim O'Donnell, Taos, NM
Text Typeset In: Perpetua

Printed in the United States of America By Cottrell Printing Company

ISBN: 978-1-7370560-7-2

THREE: A TAOS PRESS
P.O. Box 370627
Denver, CO 80237

10 9 8 7 6 5 4 3 2 1

...Like one descending

the stairs to the supply room

for a paperclip

but pausing

beneath the door frame,

a soul enters

a particular body

and cannot

remember why.

—YEHOSHUA NOVEMBER

CONTENTS

LITTLE SOUL AND THE SELVES

A BRIEF HISTORY OF WEIGHT

Start with the stillness of streets
before cars appeared, their cobblestones
worn but not fragile—it's good to do this
at dawn, mid-summer, when light
spreads like warm milk. Wait
for the hush of your own thoughts
to subside to a murmur that precedes
the language you were taught.
Let your feet relinquish the pavement,
the soil beneath, the magma beneath that
and…what else? The scarcely-perceptible
pressure of your footprints that fades so quickly
over ancient ones, and the slower fade
of a mountain or shoreline you won't notice
anyway, if you compare it to anything but itself.
Clouds are another story. They disperse
into vapor before they re-form into denser
versions of themselves to release water
so plentiful, you may begin to remember swimming
through the streets, your legs withdrawing
into nubs, then gills, back through fruited Eden
to your life as a single cell. Feeding at first
off darkness. Now you open what isn't yet an eye
and see nothing, your shape all that has been
created so far. You cast no shadow, leave no
imprint, but you tremble with your future
of replication, hint of what will later become
a clothed, coiffed, accessorized, mortgaged,
importunate body weighted with desires.

LITTLE SOUL AND THE SELVES START WITH THE STILLNESS

As to the mystery of my silence:
I remained puzzled
less by my soul's retreat than
by its return, since it returned empty-handed—
        —LOUISE GLÜCK

The Selves:

At first we didn't know it had gone—that's
the way of a three-year-old held in the lightness
every child brings into the world, babbling
without restraint, trusting all that can be touched
or tasted, fused with the universe of Self.
We had no way to comprehend a sudden onslaught
of weight—how tenacious the downward pull—
how swiftly it absorbed that lightness, another word
for Soul. Shadows lengthened over the yellow sill,
the parents laughed less, night outside the crib
was no longer friendly—so the world began to withhold
its welcome. We ceased savoring our own vowels.
Learned to shrink and sometimes vanish.
For years we had no memory of that lightness—later
no word for the small glints of its return—and no way to
reclaim or even seek what had retreated
until it was given back its name.

Little Soul:

Perhaps, the lines continue, *it is like a diver*
with only enough air in his tank
to explore the depths for a few minutes or so....
But what if, in those minutes, each foray
offers up another shard, another memory, another
glimpse of what went dark when we turned
towards the partial world that was offered us,
the rules and rewards we took over half a lifetime
to recognize as a limited source of light?
Light. Lightness. Perhaps getting older
is like learning to hold one's breath under water
and having it get easier—more backlit space
behind the eyes, more room in the little universe
of the lungs—isn't this how we began?
Seeing in the dark. Breathing under water.

LITTLE SOUL BEGINS A SERIES OF FIELD NOTES

First, it attempts to deconstruct
little. Not as in *child*. More like
background noise, backup singer on a stage
crowded with selves, girl-child
in a brace of boys, bookish, maybe
timid, maybe *muffled*, maybe
content to be left alone
until ambushed and brought to its knees
by craving. For spotlight. For the world.

Impish? Sometimes. Voice of *tickle*
or mischief, lone firefly lacing the dusk.
Or *still small voice*, whisper in someone else's ear
as counsel, old-soul wise, even as Little Soul
was put to bed too early
and was afraid of the dark.

Is it *young*? Has it been male
in other lifetimes? In this life, it has
no clue how to seek and hold dominion
(no wish, either) or what rape
has to do with desire—no trace
of ancestral testosterone, warrior
anger, singular focus, life-risking prowess....

Has it ever been *mother*? In this life
it has kept its body to itself—
inclined towards unpeopled spaces,
plants that seed themselves
when tended, river stones
sun-warmed in the palm, shy
hooved and furred creatures.

LITTLE SOUL COMES ACROSS LINES BY GEORGE SEFERIS

...and the errant soul comes to the surface
holding shards of unearthed images, a dancing girl
with useless castanets, with feet that falter,
with ankles bruised from the heavy trampling
down where the annihilated gather.

Little Soul has no ancestral memory
but knows, thanks to MyHeritage, its DNA
is pure Ashkenazi, a lineage of wanderers
and damp wool, shtetls, ghettos, rag-shops-
turned-dry-goods, bootstraps to be pulled up by,
all from a splotch of Eastern Europe
where bigotry still thrives. It had hoped for a trace
of Viking or French trapper, an aftertaste of Renaissance
or upper-crust Vienna, maybe some Romany to spice things up....

The Selves were fashioned by parents, grandparents
and great-grands educated & assimilated
in melting-pot America, accruing layers
of amnesia they wore easily as tailored sheaths
& good pearls. Christmas. Easter. Pork roasts. Cocktails
before dinner, concerts at Symphony Hall, tennis
& bridge, slipcovers in muted tweeds, mahogany
credenzas & coffee tables redolent with
lemon-oil polish.... No trace of cooking smells
from an Old Country. No raised voices, no folktales
or klezmer brass lingering in cobwebbed depths....

                    *

Little Soul can't stop thinking
about *shards of unearthed images*
and wonders how to dig for them,
how far back, reaching blind
into a murk shared with Mintz, Zeifman, Preizler,
Rekhtman, Zuckerman, Hochberg, 5th cousins
from the 2nd cousin line scattered now through
the Netherlands, Belarus, South America....
Distant fabric of losses. Shattered windows.
Books burned. Fathers taken, children
wrested from mothers, spit and yellow stars,
spirits numb with beatings, whole families erased....

but that's not it—not what happened
but how it *felt*. What does a soul carry forward
from life after life of being hated?
From relinquishments of place, of calling,
of being truly known? Inclinations. Propensities.
Recurring scripts and fears that baffle
modern parents and ambush grown-up selves.
Little Soul tends to hide
though it longs to be seen. Will move
heaven and earth to avoid being misunderstood.
Needs to be nice and is slow
to face anger. *How did it feel?*

Let some clues come forward
through image, through dream, through
meandering guess....

LITTLE SOUL ASKS THE SELVES TO COLLABORATE

on a homework assignment borrowed
from a Jungian course the Selves
are drawn to but can't afford:

Can you name three pivotal moments
in your life before the age of 18?

The course, designed to bring the Soul and ancestral
trauma, predilections, and unfinished business into the same
room and have some talks, holds scary appeal

but the Selves don't know what to look for.
They open a journal, fetch more coffee
and check email. *What is a pivotal moment?*

Reading Sophie Tucker's autobiography
at the age of seven and surprised to be understanding it?
Winning a gold-plated skating trophy in sixth grade?

Reading *The Myth of Sisyphus* in high school
and surprising the teacher by understanding it? The Selves
get up to make toast. What to do with a past

where no one starved or died, childhood
ran its course without incident, and everyone behaved?
Little Soul startles up. *That's the problem.*

No one peeked beneath appearances, no one
admitted boys were favored over girls
and no one knew what to do when Little Soul

at first had no way but bouts of sulk to express
its sense of being a stranger in a strange land, square peg
in a round hole, seeing what others

couldn't see, yet invisible in a girl-body
and branded *sensitive-bensitive*, *disagreeable*, and *insecure*
as though these were sins to be erased, not

wounds to be soothed. Little Soul gets it. The wounds
belong to unmet others waiting in the wings. Not
to the Selves—this gathering need not be a *poor me* party—

anyhow, Jung was too tough for that—
but Little Soul can't do this alone.

LITTLE SOUL REMEMBERS

before coltish legs outgrew their swiftness and supple lines

before the body lost communion with beast and tree, wind and nightfall, first snow
       and the smell of thawing soil—the body weightless, easy to forget—

before some parts began to protrude or sprout hair, the legs thickening to carry them

before seeing the flaws others might find in the relentless body

before others told the body what it was good for and what it wasn't

before the fluids, new smells, inchoate yearnings, brush of fingers

before biology and sometimes the Bible

before courtship and its consequence

before the swoon, the shroud, the dazzled senses dimming

the body welcomed and was welcomed—taking scant space, skimming
    rooftops and yards, a world laid out for the taking.

THE SELVES MAKE A STAB AT THE SECOND ASSIGNMENT

I was naturally drawn to...

Watching ink flow from mother's fountain pen over blue paper

Smell of pipe smoke, and pine needles warmed by sun

The feel of tinsel—cool, liquid between the fingers

The furry groove between our fox terrier's eyebrows

Dogs, cats, horses (real and porcelain), dinosaurs (plastic)
and once a neighbor's pet racoon sauntering by on its leash

Stones, polished or flecked with mica

Books about pioneers, collies, and older girls
good at ballet, taming horses, solving mysteries

Tchaikovsky, Johnny Mathis, The Four Seasons, Dion,
Strauss waltzes, the Kinks, the Beatles, the overture to Carmen

Cedar boxes, their scent received by small treasures

Looking at our bedroom in reverse through the dresser mirror
and seeing it afresh, its objects arranged by someone not-us

THE SELVES CHANNEL THE DAY THE PARENTS MET

I am the day mutual friends
have invited them to their wedding:
tea dance, big band music, Manhattans
and champagne. Pageboys, padded
shoulders, and wingtips. These not-
yet parents size each other up
casually, instinct not yet risen
to conscious thought (as it won't
for much of their generation
into the next) but the reptilian brain
knows, without small talk, when it meets
one of its tribe. The Big Apple sizzles
with *tempis fugit*, the country at war
with unequivocal villains far from its borders,
which means the men are heroes fighting
for what will save the entire world, and the women
have compelling jobs even if damsels
like our mother don't need them.
These parents are beautiful/handsome
as movie stars and wear clothes well.

I am prelude to the eight dates
they will have before they marry, our father
in Navy uniform and our mother in the sort of
short fur jacket one dares wear these days
and now costs nothing in thrift stores. I mark
the first day out of many they will be free
to play tennis, dance, go to theater buy
and furnish a first house, give and attend parties
that will be captured in photos captioned
in albums, prolonging their vibrant youth
until a daughter comes along and then
a son. Two blessings. Two inconveniences.
Two problems and two purposes.
Time will prove they did not make
a hasty wartime mistake, even as the years
attempt to tarnish the optimism, the patina
of charmed life, the can-do-ness and expedient
focus of their generation. I am a day suspended
in time, when America and democracy
made sense and still seemed invincible.

THE SELVES RE-INVENT A FAMILY PHOTO

The smile is genuine and wide
as the world, not the rictus we practiced
dutifully for those occasions meant
to capture a wholesome, spit-shined

family of four in America's post-war upswing
of prosperity and self-satisfaction. The hair
is not the frizz we fought, but gleaming
over an untroubled brow. We look right at the camera

as though it were new friend in a friendly world
and our little brother gazes up at us, admiring,
as he will do for the rest of our lives.
We are a girl-child who fears nothing—not

thunderstorms, reprimands, or swinging
boldly on monkey bars over the playground's
unforgiving asphalt. Our mother gazes down
at us, not at the camera—we are the center

of her world—she won't even mind when
our tonsillectomy makes her postpone a party,
a trip to New York, or theater with her bridge group.
Our father is glad we were born a girl, though this

is less clear on his face in black and white
than in our ease with frills and bows
and the crinoline skirt that doesn't itch and shoes
that don't pinch; in our face there is none

of the doubt a child picks up from adults
who don't know they've begun to learn
what we already suspect, since nothing we've said
is true: that the world is not their oyster.

THIRD ASSIGNMENT: AN ATTEMPT AT REVISION

I learned to avoid…

Firecrackers and cap guns.
Undercooked eggs.
Having our hair brushed by anyone but us.
Letting our toes touch lake muck.
Acting like a girl—wanted our father
to like us.
Being misunderstood.

Criticism—how tenaciously it lingered, smoke
from a grease fire—and so many ways
to screw up! Too loud, too blah, hair
out of control, *where's your sense of humor?*
wearing something *unbecoming*, too
serious, thin-skinned, not smart enough, not
fun, not agreeable, not *enough*….

Little Soul wonders who of the ancestors
might have hidden in wet fields and lived
on stolen eggs; who wasn't taught to read because
she was a girl; whose wild hair belied
her tribe and led to exile; who wrote books
that were burned; who was stoned
for blasphemy or miraculous healings

or dancing with abandon; who learned to survive
by erasure, by solitude, by keeping silent….
Little Soul wants to re-wire the Selves
so schooled in caution: *Maybe*
it wasn't about you.

THE SELVES DROP THROUGH THE LOOKING GLASS

into their long-ago room as though seeing it
through the eyes of, say, Lizzie Blumberg
from fifth grade staying overnight—clusters
of china terriers on one shelf, plastic palominos
and bays on another, tiny spun glass bottles
that began as a gift of one, then the Selves
collected on their own.... These arrangements,
grown nearly invisible to their meticulous
arranger, spring to action, as though from
one of Alice's Wonderland elixirs; the bay mare
now faces her colt from the left instead of right;
the tallest glass swirl stands sentry over the smaller
confections, all of them gilded in lamplight
slanting from opposite its usual corner—
and then there's the desk, cedar pencil box and pink
eraser placed with surprising neatness beside the blotter
as though by a model student with round handwriting,
and a gap in the row of books revealing where *Jane Eyre*
was pulled out and now lies face-down on the bed....
Ah, the *bed*—suddenly nestled alongside
an unfamiliar wall, below a window that offers
the neighbors' yard in reverse—what unexpected dreams
might gather there? What stories might the dreamer
begin about herself and actually finish?

LITTLE SOUL ON THIN ICE: A HISTORY OF NAVIGATION

On the forest preserve's midwinter lake
I clung to my parents' hands. Every
step I tried on the double runners
turned my legs into strangers,
mean things whose taunts
I couldn't predict. Only my hands
belonged to me, hanging on. The ice
was an unfamiliar world, shocking
as thunder, or the chlorinated water
that once closed over my head
and crushed me with silence.

                    *

Watching my father shave
before the mirror, his hands
so sure and his skin a burnished
tan over muscle, I thought his body
was an unbroken law. Fevers

never came to him like punishment.
He could swim the length of the neighbors' pool
underwater. He could fix lamps and cars and toilets
and once, from a cigar box, built a stage-prop
Geiger counter full of knobs and flashing lights.

I never told anyone of the water
that kept filling my mouth.
I didn't know where it came from
or what had broken. I didn't
know there was a word, *saliva*.

*

My parents glided easily, laughing
and upright, as though the ice
were just another form of ground.

*

How is it I've come to embrace
the dance that is skiing?—the tenuous
bargain between gravity and
trust—pushing the edge of too fast
until I can bail out only by shifting my fear
from foot to foot, one steering me
out of the fall-line while the other
tries to steer clear of my brain flashing
frozen tree, cracked bone, stained snow....

For years I have pitched myself against
the hardest trails, pitching myself in truth
against the spinster-child who lives in me
still, with her chapped nose and skinny calves,
hiding from the world with a book
in her hand and an afghan over her knees....
How did I come to embrace the winter landscapes
we've traveled all these years—

the ice and exposed rock, the blinding powder,
the drop-offs, tree wells, moguls?—sometimes
we fly off a lip and become for a moment
weightless, incandescent, our future thrillingly
on hold. Looking down from the chairlift,
we pluck at one another's sleeve and can't
imagine *hearth glow*, can't imagine *dry socks*
or *sweet steam of cocoa*, can't imagine how
I'm going to get us down that hill again.

LITTLE SOUL GOOGLES MERWIN'S TRANSLATION OF HADRIAN'S ANIMULA

Little soul little stray
little drifter
now where will you stay
all pale and all alone
after the way you used to make fun of things

Little Soul might do well to befriend
this naughty doppelganger, this
maker-of-mischief, passer-of-notes-
behind-the-Don's back, irrepressible
flirt, wedding-crasher guzzling
two champagnes before it slips to yet
another rented hall to run a finger
along a rim of tiered cake while no one's looking. . . .
Animula, Alma—why the feminine endings?—
why the implicit *sugar-and-spice*?
Little Soul would do well to misbehave
now and then—find out how it would
feel, for example, to be a Tom Jones
seducing the young Baroness, then slipping
away, buttoning its trousers in the nick of time
laughing. Unrepentant. Unencumbered.

When Doubt Takes Shape and Weight

it wakes the dreamer to a body
filled with lead. Repaints

the past, blurring landscapes where
soul wandered unencumbered by self

and foregrounding dismissals, shards
of scorn, misogynies flung carelessly

long ago, real and imagined
failures settling like old snow

over the nuances of true
memory, if such a thing exists....

What purpose these
visitations, this recurrent crumbling?

What would appease it—
a quilt to burrow in? Soup

fragrant with marrow and herbs?
Someone to lead it to the hearth

and whisper, *Take this cup, this*
firelight, this haven, this

still hour. Take the seeds. Leave
the grit. Wait for a rune——an accurate

correction——to glitter up from the leavings.
Take this listening, this mirror

that might gather and hold you.

WHO CAME WHEN? NOTES FROM A PHONE CONVERSATION HELD TOO LATE

Father's side

      Germany   mid 1800's   driven away   conscription of Jewish farmers

                    rural Wisconsin

Paternal grandfather   timberland   horse barns (draft and gaited)

          pillar of rural Antigo (only Jew)

                went to Congregational church

        Lost everything (the Depression, rise of the automobile)

          Chicago suburb   Success at an in-law's brokerage firm

            Well-appointed home   His losses

                   came with him

   His sister (Great-aunt Bea)

         high-end clothing store   Appleton   (a city then?)

                 (Clientele? Wealthy farmers' wives?)

Paternal grandmother   finishing school in Chicago   Europe with chaperone

     Hull House with Jane Adams   designed fine silver (Arts & Crafts movement)

           eleven siblings

      one died in front of her after hunting (gun accidently went off)

          another—a parent?—a suicide   she

              found the body

              *

Mother's side

        Nuremberg (family plot there)   mid 1800's

Opa's mother   Bertha ("Birdie")   "a great beauty"   Elgin, IL

Opa's father   Isaac   Descended from tinkers??

Opa   New York, age 3   Cornell   Columbia (law)

 Oma's grandfather   Salt Lake City   possible spellings (Hirshman?
          Hirschmann? Hirshman/n? Hershmann?)
              sold miner's equipment   hid Brigham Young in their basement

    Oma's mother—Little Soul knew her—
       Victorian   looked like George Washington
     obsessed with bowel functions and imminent disasters
        if-you-pick-your-nose-you'll-look-like-Pinocchio
           don't-put-that-in-your-mouth-it-has-germs
               (the Selves were scared of her)

    Oma   Chicago   jeweled brooches   vodka cocktails   apple-smoked bacon
        Collected recipes   never cooked
          never left home until Wellesley   never had learned how
             to make a bed

Seen and Not Heard

Oma did not dote. She did not cuddle
or coo. She traveled the world as the wife
of a lawyer/diplomat and at home
gave dinner parties that required
four sets of dishes, three of crystal.
She wore tailored tweeds and, to tamp
stubborn curl, a hairnet and helmet of spray.

Brought the Selves a miniature
gilt coach from the Queen's coronation,
read them *Grimm's Fairy Tales*,
sang "The Owl and the Pussycat" a little
off-key, and spoke to the Selves
as though they were adults. Did not
suffer fools, her dry wit directed
somewhere over their heads; intimidated
at first, Little Soul came to like it.

She was raised strictly,
according to custom of class
and era, by immigrant help in a well-
appointed nursery, taking meals with her brother
and entering the world through reading.
Likewise, Little Soul's mother and aunt
were trotted out to shake hands
with guests and then discreetly led away.
On fine days they were taken to Central Park
by their nanny, who taught them a few
German words and how to sew.

She carried needlepoint and at least
one book everywhere—a private world
to keep close?—and loved opera.
Once, late in life, she confessed to Little Soul
that if she could come back she wanted
to be a soprano—maybe coloratura—
and *whoosh*, Little Soul took in the secret
soar, the longing, the untapped
limelight and calling.

THE SELVES GO TO ISRAEL

summer after high school
    kibbutz
         southern swatch of Negev   the Six-Day War
                still
            two years away
two months
    the dry heat a force
                    embraceable
everyone in their twenties
            no hierarchies
                no rules
                    mornings in the orchards
            no temple
            no Hebrew recitations
            Saturday Shabbat their Sunday

cool evenings   soft grass outside the library
        singing with someone's guitar   discussing books
                The 1812 Overture on a turntable
                              canons
                                  & brass & cymbals
                            almost sexual
                the stars
                    flaring & fading overhead
        to bed at after midnight   rise before dawn
            (nap all afternoon)

Helen, owner of a scrap of dog named Oscar saying
        (apropos of what?)...*but you don't have to worry, you're pretty*
  out of the blue
              revelation
                    far from home
                            a fresh mirror
turning down
                chances to
                    lose their virginity
                        to Byronic chain-smoking Johnny White
      feeling unfinished

      exhilarating light
                the sky
                a furnace
watering fig trees
    wrapping mesh to keep caterpillars off
                        the ripening fruit

LITTLE SOUL AND THE SELVES GO ON A SECOND TRIP

two years after the Six-Day War
(the Selves' dream job
New York fashion magazine
first step to a future)
before the right-wingers bruised
the empathic soul   the young nation
not yet entrenched
Arab sector of Jerusalem newly
reclaimed
red embroidery on white muslin
haunches of meat hanging in the sun   flies   hawkers
the Selves photographed in wool mini-dress   (Bedouin & his camel
nearby for color)
Little Soul leaning towards escape
(a Vespa through the Old City
with gentle Sol
threads of light behind shutters
narrow streets   smoky
unknowable lives
every door a mystery
an alley   a bakery
fresh bagels spongy & fragrant at 2 a.m.)
Tour bus
catered lunches
dignitaries   cocktails   Tel Aviv   Jerusalem
everything preserved on contact sheets
autumn layers & wool scarves for the August issue
(even in the desert)

Little Soul nostalgic for

   kibbutz & cottons worn soft from the laundry

    Avi or Ephraim playing accordion after dinner

     stars unhampered by lights   horizontal vistas

    New York looming as wrong fit

& sat in the rear with the guide asked about his life

   wrote down lyrics to Israeli folk songs

    fingered edges of inchoate dream away from dream job

 while the Selves sat with the others

   chattering oblivious in wool New York-bound

   years away from comprehending

     the about-face brewing at the back of the bus

SEMINAL ENCOUNTERS WITH POT

The first time, a room full of strangers,
how does one inhale, nothing happening
for several tokes, then a terror-
cloud, burgeoning. The fireplace
yawns ember and smoke,
the crunch of potato chips
sends boulders tumbling through the brain
but worst is The Chandler Brothers' "Time"
filling the room with electric-guitar
keening, tick-tock percussion an evil heartbeat,
and Little Soul slips down a rabbit hole of echoes
to a point of no return, leaving the Selves
to cope: daughter on a blind date, college girl
trying to be cool, primal creature staring
at the fire in a cave of threats wondering
when, how, she will get home.

Years later. Little Soul and the Selves
alone at home with cigarette papers
and a baggie left by a guest, *how does one
roll this?* and Kitaro on the stereo
spilling New Age progressions into
story, journey, pleasant conversation
that requires no effort. Trail mix, sweet-
savory explosions in the mouth—
Little Soul and the Selves are having
a party! The Selves have forgotten
their social masks (new professional, collegial
cocktailer, recent divorcee-doing-just-fine-thank you)
and Little Soul forgets to be reticent.
Everyone's in pj's. Savoring the music's
turns of plot, and how raisins
and salted almonds play well together

as do Little Soul and the Selves
discovering layer by layer, as the evening
unspools ribbons of revelation, how much they
like each other. Can converse or be silent.
Can watch each other's backs—perhaps
they have done so all along, this trust
having waited in the wings.

THE SELVES ASK LITTLE SOUL FOR HELP

with the fourth assignment: *My homelife taught me…*

To keep our impressions to ourselves.

To forget our impressions.

To become good at fashioning masks and wearing them:
dutiful student, polite to mother's friends, adequately but not too
popular, not flashy, not promiscuous, never out of control,
normal, normal to the point of avoiding censure
and being years away from knowing who we were.

Little Soul feels a cloud of purpose
taking shape. Then it glows as though touched
from beneath by late sun. Swelling inside / outside,
edging out shame, and filling the hollow
of *misunderstood. Invisible. Unfinished. Unsayable——*

what if, after all, Little Soul and the Selves are here to
heal not-self? What if they are repaying the parents,
who nurtured as best they knew, by picking up
the baton they didn't know they carried——
misunderstood, unfinished, unsayable——

and carrying it closer to the finish line?

LITTLE SOUL, EXPATRIATE

i

Bogotá: Why I Felt Safe

Because I wore no gold or faceted stones.
Because I walked quickly in low-heeled shoes
and looked straight ahead, as though a kitchen or
office pulled me toward tasks too common
to be noticed, a tunnel encasing me in apparent blandness.
Because I carried green and white grocery bags
that said, "Carulla" full of vegetables, bread, and detergent.
Because my real life and language were far away, making
small things large—young women on their lunch break
laughing on the street, businessmen glancing up
from coffee to exchange newspaper sections, scenes
much like home, but for the strange language
pelting me in a rain of small stones.

Other expats had stories of a purse snatched from
a car, wallet missing at a restaurant, diamond stud
torn from an ear. And the papers at home mentioned
bombs in the library, smashed windows at the embassy,
kidnapped millionaires, universities closed down.
Whenever I saw crowds milling or shouting, I walked
around the edges, the diminished wavelets. I walked
for the sensation of briskness, like others who broke away
for a meeting, the hairdresser, a bowl of *casuela*.

Every afternoon, wearing leotards under street clothes,
I got on a bus in a crush of commuters, carrying
my emptiness the way each clerk, shopper, and mother
carried in her head a little map of plans. I got off
two blocks from a dance studio where I leaned into Spanish
with my whole slowed self, stretching until my muscles
filled my head like conversation, and watched
my limbs in the mirror trying to repeat into phrases
the steps the instructor was making.

Later I came back to the same door
with its two locks—keys in one hand, groceries
in the other. I had long stopped thinking of home.
The bones of my face had lost definition, the nuances
of my very thoughts had flattened with no one to hear them—
who would harm someone like that?

ii

For a time the Spanish Language

was fruit too high to reach—
I could only grasp a few low-hanging
globes, many not yet ripe. *Si, gracias, por favor,*
que tengue un buen dia, me llamo....
The cornucopia that had been my mind—its nuances,
its promising buds of digression and speculation—
withered in the streets, on busses, in front of Carulla's
vast display of produce as Spanish, a cascade
of green, red, yellow sweetness, flowed around me
and deepened my silence. *Piña*, pineapple; *manzana*,
apple; *naranjo*, orange; *queso fresco*, the salty white cheese
to put on cream crackers (for me, the taste of Bogotá
the way camembert on a crisp baguette had been
the taste of Paris). I spent most days talking to myself,
my native tongue losing its timbre. For one hour
each afternoon, the landlady's daughter came to tutor me
in filling a prescription, asking directions, discussing
American novels, getting the typewriter fixed.
I learned to rearrange phrases in my head so I could
graft to them what little Spanish I had. Little by little
a few words began to hang within reach, ripe for the picking.
One day I tasted them as they formed in my mouth,
my mind still under-utilized and mostly snuffed—but oh
the burst of sensation, the senses coming to life, the hollow
that had been my mouth suddenly filled with something
sun-warmed and sweet. The taste of Spanish.

iii
Sometimes I think I dreamed

the horses of Colombia, along with the stream
that flowed through the middle of a cottage
I visited once, in the mountains, for a dinner of rose-
colored fish steamed on palm leaves over a fire
and the tailored matron I met on a bus, who
seemed to see straight into my unsettled heart
and gave me a necklace of brown coral

but especially the snowy Arabian whose tail
swept the ground, whose mane flowed like silk
over my hands. The breeder who let me ride him
dismissed him for his imperfect gait; his specialty
was Peruvian Paso Finos, fine-boned as deer,
necks thickened from training to hold their heads
high and tucked, their trot so smooth a rider
could carry a full cup of water without spilling.

Such acquiescence, such flare, such tender
muzzle and deep lake of eye—every Christmas
fat men who bought the Paso Finos
drank too much *aguardiente* and rode them
in a parade from *El Centro* to the outskirts of Cali
slouching, listing starboard to port, until they
tipped their slender mounts to the pavement.

And the *paseo* I went on one day, my horse
an over-trained jumper from the country club
catapulting me through fields and rivers—did I dream
this too?—hours of hard riding with no cool-down,
a portly man's chestnut mare found collapsed, dead,
as a fleet of waiters cleared the remains of *sancocho*
de gallina and *arepas* we had eaten under the trees.

For a few moments that Arabian was mine,
a cloud gleaming beneath me, his springy jog
easy to sit. I dreamed his owner let me take him north
over several borders, in dark boxcars and trailers
lit by those flanks. I dreamed us floating along
the ditch banks where I lived, ranchers in pickups
startled by Pegasus in the flesh, moonlight
on marble, *Arabian Nights* in West Texas.

Little Soul Contemplates Skin as the Largest Organ of the Body

Smooth wing singing on air—
in bed at night I would start
the story, *Once there was a little girl…*
but couldn't think what came next.
I wanted to be heard by

everyone in my life exactly as I
sounded to myself, *wing, singing,* but the words
kept imploding like the fragile
soap bubbles I tried to blow gently
to the top of our elm—so I'd pretend

I was Davy Crockett, wounded
in the shoulder, finally resting, certain
the Alamo would hold, and my faithful
horse would soon carry me home.
I must have wanted to wrap myself

in something that would bend
but not break as I moved through
the day's white water—the reprimands
and questions, large people coming
in and out of any room to bump

against my thoughts—the way I imagined
a cloud would hold, if I landed from a great
height—a little giving ground, a little
firm sky. I must have been seen as a sulky kid,
a walking scab, and wanted just to get by.

From the valley that cradles me now
I straighten up and peer over the rim
like the sun. I touch my shoulder. It's
nearly healed. And the heart? A sapling.
A flowering. An old tree full of nests....

For the child who couldn't find
an ending but learned to build poems
out of twigs, I breathe a *thanks*
long in coming—and for the mountain
that keeps its shape beneath swaths

of fog—and for the friends
who have breathed their stories
over mine, flowing in and out
of homes I have lived in,
the walls inhaling and exhaling

to hold us—and for the tall horse
that has carried me along dunes
and ditch banks, giving me something
like wings, though he is sometimes
afraid of shapes in the wind.

SOUL-MAKING: SIX LESSONS IN LOVE

i

Saying Goodbye

always takes too long or too short, regardless
of time spent thinking about it, turning
and turning away, opening one window
after another to let fresh air into
the self, that neglected house, after a holiday—

for in the end, the words are a one-time
performance. Even when that lover suddenly
isn't around, they gather the way clouds do,
his evasions drifting into silence until you, too
have nothing real to say.

It happens after you've stayed too long
in his wrecked country where lies are bread
and meat, yearly rain, hard cash, safe
conduct. To answer a question straight
was to shred your passport at the border

and bare your pockets to thieves—but oh, how
you loved those the nights under stars, the speaking
with hands, the toxic and intoxicating local brew—
stories that required obtuseness from you as a form of
good manners. Now, after weeks alone, you still

find ourself roused from sleep some nights
trying and failing to explain it all away. Pain
is a raven clinging to your shoulder. Eventually
it happens like this: you head into the beverage section
of the local grocery, and there he is, buying wine

and holding someone else's hand. You walk forward
in slow motion, a little curious. His eyes slide
right past you, as though he were scanning the aisle
for yet another woman, and his hair is short now,
trimmed close as a convict's. He steers her

away, pretending you never appeared, and it's
the pretense that makes *goodbye* flare into fertile
finality—the pretense that makes you notice
his greenish look from too much bad
water—the pretense that lifts the bird's wings

and lets you fly home for good.

ii
Borrowed

Say, he is Pan with gentle hands,
his eyes creased with mischief—
he likes to roam at night, nothing
but him and the stars, his blue gaze
bright in his sleepless face. He says
he wants to grow old with you

though he must keep you, and have you
keep yourself, a secret. You know precisely
at what point the pain will begin if he
keeps coming around, calling your name
softly in the pre-dawn stillness.

Say, he has kissed you once, then slipped
away, flushed and dizzy, to the element
he brought with him, the scent of night
and the unsetting light of a sinking moon.
Say, you've made love once, and again he has
vanished into the last tendrils of darkness.

By day he drives to work across the border
to cut steel with a needle of flame—you can see
him draping his arm along the truck's open window,
his skin browning in the sun—and later treats kindly
the woman he says he wants to stop living with.

At night your own house holds a throng of memories
as echoes of other men who once thought you
a discovery or the one person who understood them
find their way in, along with grit from spring's first
furious winds—sometimes it's your ex muttering
worthless, glowering and refusing to talk

though he's told others he never stopped
loving you—you left him and don't want to
go back, but lately you curl over the part of yourself,
as though from a blow, where love for him
drove a deep root. And see how you
turned and turned from that greenness

until it dried, withered, and settled to ash.
You trace its residue, nights alone, while
this other man is whistling or stirring gravy
or washing the dog, seamless and easy
in his double life. One morning you're easing

your skittery mare from the barn, tears
filling your eyes for no reason, like blood
washing dirt from a wound, when he appears
in the doorway, the sun behind him,
his hair where your hands
may or may not rest a bright nest

spun against hard daylight—say, he is
Mercury—Hermes—messenger riding
the thermals—say, he's another crack in a heart
that yearns, as hearts tend to do, in spring's
restless weather—perhaps this time

it will leave a scar like soldered gold.
Seared, then annealed. Perhaps, you hope,
the seasons finally will get through to you
with their simple lesson: subtraction
& replacement, the earth's loose skin
stripping itself again & again.

iii
Sisters

Reading a friend's blog about her ill-fated
adventures with married men, I wonder
about the wives, those background stick figures,
their inner landscapes conveniently erased
along with their once-loved faces smiling
or tear-stained, beseeching or crumpled, their
hopes and burdens banished from the snow-
globe world of a man and woman mistaking
lack of scruples for freedom. Erotic *chutzpah*.
The right to search and seize.

But twice, long ago, I fell there myself, not
knowing at first the men were partnered and then,
once I knew, electing to seize—what?—not
a point to prove, but something that might
put me fully in my skin as never before. What
possessed me? Not arrogance. Greed? Ignorance
for sure, which might as well have been my own
snow-globe of need, closing me in and blurring
my view of the landscape of burdened, steadfast
wives I once glimpsed at a distance

and dismissed—by a me much younger,
working out my own story, not ready to
imagine anyone else's. I cringe now, still
not knowing what I would say to those women
who knew those two men better than I ever would.
I hope one of them is happy with her
Peter Pan whom I loved for a time, and I hope
the other is free of the man whose PTSD mowed down
everything in its path. I am sorry, Catherine and Sarah.
There was so, so much my unfinished heart

wasn't yet pummeled and stretched enough to hold.

iv

Intimacy

…needs a sign on the wall that says "Unbalanced Load"
          —KATHLEEN STEWART AND LAUREN BERLANT

Consider, yes, the invisible lumps and shifts
of what someone you live with is trying
to batten down as he/she opens the blinds, starts
the coffee, fills the cat bowl—but what about
the stash of memories, triggers, and withheld
retorts you haven't figured out what to do with,
rattling around in the oversized flatbed
of your inner life? You never know what will clog
a day's routine commerce, requiring frequent
stops, the tightening of bungee cords,
just to keep up civilized conversation
and play by tacit rules. Or break the rules
if a conversation you need to have gets detoured
or pulled over before it can deliver—
sometimes you need time to wander around
for the right question, or a version of truth
that will not upend the baggage another self
is hauling. So consider the load times-two. Both
in the same lane tailgating, passing one another
by a hair, hubcaps and fenders kissing the air.

v

Solitude Switch

If a woman is lucky to live alone
long enough to like it, the wiring is set
despite the later luck and benign
static of sharing space with a loved
mate whose packing for a brief trip

now brings on temporary panic—*What
will I do if the pilot light goes out?*—
and mourning his absence on the other side
of the bed even while he's
still in it….

*Sociality is a query into what others
are doing and know,* said one of two women
who dialogued in brief essays, long-
distance, exchanging ironies and icy humor,
each riff sparked by the keenness of the other's

refusal to take for granted common behaviors
they isolate and probe, each observation
almost graspable though undercut in a flash
by the next, so that reading them is like
running one's fingers over broken glass.

Now, first day alone, my dreamy
ignorance returns, their printed words
settling into a blank-slate mind and
mulled over during light cleaning
and routine chores, the unsocial air

an old slipper easy to slip into
and pad around in, the hours
losing their shape. Eating
from a saucepan. Summoning
the patience to ease the tight screw-top

off the Pinot Grigio. Locating
and resetting a tripped fuse.
Remembering, though my better
half indeed leaves a gap, a dormant
half is still wired in.

vi
Virginal

Not so much *chaste*
as how one emerges from
the roiled sheets touched, yes, at one
petaled place but not all the lotus
openings—heart, throat, third eye,
seats of utterance and insight.

Not derailed, not surrendered, not
disembodied—though the Little Soul understands
that such transports exist for some
women possessed of sublime erotic
skills and sensibility—something the Selves
aspired to, for a time.

Sensual, maybe...
warm fur stroking skin as the cat
emerges from beneath the covers, sun-
sweet apple just shaken from the tree,
moonstone refracting hints of lavender
and yes, the warmth and male firmness
of a soulmate's hand encountered
late in life. His clear eyes across the table.
His solid shoulders. Ease in passing one another
naked or clothed in shared rooms. *Intimacy*.

Still, Little Soul remains a semi-wild
creature nourished in solitude, the presence
of animals, the new scents of earth at the cusp

of each season. Deaf to pick-up lines, no longer
swayed by the plumage and promise of
courtship (the Selves, for a time, experimented)....
Artemis. Atalanta. Peter Pan in a girl's body.
Friend of men, yes. Lover of one. The core
intact.

No Mask or Gloves, Please

when handling words
as finger paint. Wet clay. Watercolor
that refuses to replicate
the obvious. Mess
and color. Serendipity. Under
the fingernails. Outside
the lines. Little Soul
wants them plastic
and spiraled. Moments
that hold silence against gusts
of everyone else's noise. Sometimes
the keyboard is both palette
and piano, the fingers and wrists
supple above it—lit up, practiced,
flitting with spontaneous collage
and choreography. Little Soul seeks
(and sometimes finds) words
free of *thinking*, like a long run
in nippy air, or a dance
with a sexy stranger.

After Dancing

there lingers, for a while,
a certain grace—endorphins
zinging, male and female
in one body fully met and free
of yearning—the aftertaste
of mastery and intricate
collaboration. Touch and response,
tango / quickstep / dip-and-twirl, the Selves
swept into every nuanced move
and astonished that they know, better-
late-than-never, how to flirt. How
to follow a guide from without until it
lodges within. Then Little Soul and the Selves
drive home alone, humming a little Sinatra,
and float into the shower, then to bed
and wake the next morning
still lit up from having done
something they were meant for
and remembering the sequins, the sweat,
the steadying hand *Let's do this again*
while the world spun around them.

LITTLE SOUL, STONE-WHISPERER

Gemstones have their own
dialects, as do cubic zirconia, Czech
crystal, rondelles of antler and abalone.

There's sunstone, harboring peach chips and mica—
and turquoise, veined with the darkness of its origins
against its own luminous sky. Agate is turned earth
and old greens; carnelian, melted caramel; opal, live
coals. They let you know which stones they do

and do not want to converse with, the way fire shrinks
from *water*, or *air* feeds flame, though *earth*
is their congenial matrix—if we could see underground
who knows what bedazzlement thrives in the dark?
When I string them I have to listen. Stay out of their way.

Coral, moonstone, aquamarine—red glisten
of melon, cool orb glowing on a clear night, Caribbean
waters lit by noon… Lately, labradorite
draws me into snow-laden cloud, a little sunlight
seeping through—it asks to be placed next to

garnet and rose quartz. I'm not in charge—
if they don't like what I've done, I have to
unstring the whole conversation and start again.

Each Plant Soul Honored

Consider the stunted
yarrow seedling lifted from a crack
in asphalt before a neighbor's impeccably
landscaped plot—an escapee
thriving against the odds—I dug it out
with a teaspoon to save it from tires,
put it in the smallest pot I had

and was sure I should keep it
indoors over the winter. *Not so*,
said the expert in October. It needs
hard freeze, short daylight and snow—
never mind the flattened, browned stems
and withered leaves. Never mind how diminished
it looks in the modest plot. *Plant it outdoors
now*. Today, six months later, I had to
untangle it from the lilies and cosmos
and cut it back. *To be rooted is perhaps
the most important and least recognized
need of the human soul*, said Simone Weil.

Little Soul Drops into the Waiting

screen as into a mantra,
eyes turned inward, to receive
something like respite
from *words*—a floating,
wash of unfocussed—if one
can call it—*thought*, while the sun
climbs its ladder, and trucks
outside churn their way to the condo-
construction site up the mountain.
Another day of climbing. Of small
arrivals. Engine and errand, lists
and crossings-off. And in the news
another conspiracy theory, another
stalled climate fix, another gerrymandered
denial of what the populace wants
brought strident to light as though
for the first time. This morning
the petunias and vinca watered yesterday
need help again, the sun having pulled
all moisture from gallon pots. August
heat and little rain like every year,
mornings of pitcher and sprinkler, filling
and emptying, dishwasher and fridge,
dirty and clean.... What if history itself
is a simple continuum of dissolution and
solution, error and insight, despair
and repair?—might the pummeled soul
of a self, a country, find solace in that?

If Little Soul and the Selves Were a Rock Band

today is the sort of day
they would slip out of the tour bus
with its empty wrappers and plastic forks,
wander into strange neighborhoods, peer
into windows and pretend they can sit
with a book as long as they wish beside
this tiffany lamp, spend an afternoon
with iced tea in the Adirondack chair under *that*
maple, eat scrambled eggs and toast on a white plate
at a glimpsed kitchen island before heading
to class with new notebooks and pencils
or burrow into a duvet at night behind shutters
now propped open to catch the first cool
lick of autumn——never mind
spring fever, what about that first
lift of summer's heavy air, scent of
something dry burning safely as trees release
windfalls, and later the astonishing silence
of first snow? Little Soul and the Selves
don't want to do their do-wop thing today,
don't want to sing their little back-up hearts out
dreaming themselves on the cover of *Rolling Stone*——
yes they're a team, yes they yearn, but today
they want to drift inside the mystery of other lives,
what they can remember and what they can
invent, as another season that once seemed endless
tilts surreptitiously towards the next.

DO-WOP DESTINY

Some people will do anything
to be famous and there are other
people who just will sing.
   —LISA FISHER

The cadence of names—
   Martha and the Vandellas
     Country Joe and the Fish
       Smoky and the Miracles
        The Raelettes The Ikettes
and the caramel bridge or gospel soar of
   backup singers clustered around one microphone
      their miniskirts and teased hair a veneer
        the ageless flights and depths of voice
  (now forgotten)
    pruning their bloom
      to *the blend*—

Little Soul and the Selves
   likewise incline—
     one letting the Chairman blow off steam
      then softly
      mapping middle ground
        smoothing ruffled
        tempers

    one a not-guru in the classroom
     intent on drawing out
       the quiet ones until they hear
        themselves
   one tamping Dionysian exuberance
    in a zoot-suit jitterbug
      to follow
       feather-light
        the exacting partner—

and have regrets   the tact

the "light touch"

the very *blend* sometimes

a chafing that forms black pearl

luminous & deep

longing

handed down as   *birthright?*

Perhaps some ancestor

rarely seen in the village

charged with the flock

keeping drift & shape together

offered his music to sky

honing the instrument

adding octaves

listening, always listening

lived & died

almost

satisfied.

Little Soul Takes a Day Off

from Soul-searching—thinking, screen-
and-typing time—instead, yoga in the park
followed by aimless errands (two grocery stores
to find a pair of rubber gloves), deadheading petunias,
brushing the cats, several visits to the fridge
and continual cracking of the neck grown tight—what's
trapped in there, anyway? An unparsed code?
A whitewashed past? The meridians send flares,
a run helps but not the Audible book
depicting scenes from Ravensbruck where
not even the guards escaped unspeakable damage.
Little Soul, relieved of its duty to make an appearance,
has retreated to time before memory, before
trackable history, perhaps before humankind
made cruelty a calling—to spend the day
harvesting datura, knapping flint, and painting
aurochs and bison on cave walls that will
not be found for 30,000 years.

LITTLE SOUL AND THE SELVES DIVERGE ON THE ISSUE OF MASKS

The Selves are proud of their knack for protective
coloration: in Paris they managed to "casually" drape
a scarf and were thrilled when a man in a Citroen
pulled up to ask directions; in Bogotá they wore
shell earrings, carried a purse of coarse woven yarns
and no one took them for an easy mark; wore black
in Milan; embroidered shirts in Oaxaca; on the Altiplano
a poncho that still smelled of llama. The trick: to not
dress American, just as in college they sought to not
look Jewish, grateful for blue eyes and a harmless
surname, and in grad school full of edgy, tormented
writers they kept their mouths shut about their lack
of debt, lack of lovers, and still-married parents.

For a time, Little Soul and the Selves spend their not-
home time in masks—patterned cloth, blue pleated
paper, and once a contraption fashioned from half
a vacuum cleaner bag. They agree on this gesture
of civic fealty, along with the reduced chance
of spreading or receiving something akin to
what their father called *the screamin' crud.*
None of them minds being taken for Liberals
because they are. The times call for renegotiations
between Self and World—Little Soul and the Selves
are ready to engage. And to be conversing
freely with each other during this time
of no travel, no girls' nights or house guests

—which is why Little Soul feels, for the first time, expansive
behind its mask. More four-cornered every day.
Lit with small revelations.

LITTLE SOUL CONTEMPLATES THE BRAIN AS UNIVERSE

7:00 am, and the assertive high-desert sun
it's accustomed to is socked away by leaden clouds—
rather, Little Soul is socked in, lamps kindled

against the murk, the body slow to awaken
and the mind millstone gray. The brain, according
to experts in Mindfulness and PT, is surprisingly

fixable —skilled guidance can bypass or re-direct
the damaged circuits. *Neuroplasticity*.
As though that wrinkled mass were translucent

and easy to warm, soften, and re-rearrange
for less encumbered dialogues within itself
via a system of discernable laws. Something akin

to mathematics. But what of *personality*, that swirl—
that underworld—that mess—of memories,
longings, triumphs, grudges, ambivalent

forgiveness …? Little Soul imagines something watery,
uncontained, like light in a Turner painting—blue lagoon
of brooding, or white-capped with outrage,

or awash in shame the texture and color
of fog that muffles the sharp ridge of El Salto
even as sunlight begins to seep through.

THE SOUL KNOWS HOW TO MOURN

while Self keeps lists and answers
email and makes a hair appointment. Asks
the waiter that's inside the dim sum
at the next tale. The soul wants to sit
on a low stool, speak only when spoken to
and allow a seven-day river of memories
and tears to cleanse it for a future without him
but Self won't allow this, Self thinks
it can run on fumes, so here I am, without
my father a month now, on and off planes,
speaking more than listening, checking
something else off the list as the dam in my throat
closes and my voice disappears, the voice I
lean on, the soul shutting down the blind machine.

LITTLE SOUL TAKES ON T.S. ELIOT

So the darkness shall be the light, and the stillness the dancing.
        —T.S. ELIOT

I said to my soul be still—but who
gives it such council, admonishing
a part of himself whose judgement

he apparently does not trust—a *soul*
not fit to *love* or have *faith in* any
but the *wrong thing*—how has

this mortal, steeped in education
and entitlement, come to regard
his *soul* as twitchy, unfinished,

malleable as a child bride?
Blindsided. Hot-housed. Listened-to
and revered. Fluent in assertions

but now, I'm guessing with arrogance
of my own, weary, the undertow of age
having put the brakes on heedless desire

and headlong possibility—wasn't he
once a child, a tender thing that dwelt
easily with silence, the core of him

quiet, self-nourishing and joyous
before the world closed in and shaped it
male?—here I am, patronizing Eliot

for patronizing his soul which I can't
help but think grasped all along
the sanctuary of *stillness*, the flights

it offered, the choreography
of doing nothing and then receiving
whatever poured in…. I wonder if

his soul, having never relinquished
its nimble footwork or the music of silence,
may have stepped in to admonish *him* in this poem.

Little Soul Once Wanted to Travel Incognito

Blue eyes. An unremarkable
nose. Assimilated precedents. No knowledge
of Hebrew. A surname that could belong to
any German living many generations in white-bread
America. . . . Sometimes I glimpse briefly in the mirror
the melancholy cast of a grandmother's eyes,

the one who had eleven siblings and whose mother
took her own life. Sometimes I see an uncle's
sensitive, wistful mouth, the one inclined
towards music and art, who bailed on a law degree
and sold sporting goods in order to provide.
As I age, I see my face morphing

into something androgynous, assertive
of cheekbone and nose, no longer pretty or
tentative, like the faces of wealthy Jewish
patrons of the symphony or opera or PBS.
My skin tans easily. I am drawn to meditation,
Yoga, and the possibility of reincarnation

because it explains better than any faith
I've explored, any service I ever attended,
why we come into the world, what purpose
our trials serve, and what may await us
next. I don't know what to make of God—
this actually is very Jewish where I

live now, an historic high-desert town
that has long harbored communes, New Age
celebrities, aging hippies and spiritual seekers—
Jew-Buhs is the word for the many Jews here
now turned Buddhist. Others are Unitarians,
atheists, Jungians.... Escapees, all of us perhaps,

sharing the land with descendants of Spaniards
who fled the Inquisition to settle among natives
whose land this was—is—their adobe metropolis
still standing after 1000 years.... I feel at home
in this mix, its tensions and reconciliations, its
take and give—and no longer care what I don't

look like, though once, still groping through murk
for a self I could count on, I very much did.

LITTLE SOUL OFF THE HOOK

 The Critic slides from my shoulder,
drained of her hoarse caw of a voice,
her dark plumage dragging the ground.
I have taken away her arsenal
of quibbles, conditions, and the ongoing

list of people she insists I can't
win over. I am a garden, abloom in the dark
all these years. And the people who raised me?
Well-meaning cyphers, stick figures
against a crowded horizon—how did I

keep it up, channeling their voices, amping
the volume until my shortcomings
slapped me into action like shots of expresso?
Lately she can't even lift her hand to wave
as I drift off in a cloak of near-invisibility,

immune to the seduction of another
impossible task—once I sent poems
into the world like arks in a storm bearing
some urgent message on behalf of a hijacked self—
once I reached towards a man's starved cheek

while his eyes drifted to someone waiting
behind me. And to someone waiting
behind that someone. What now?
I learn the pleasures of *mull*
and *putter* because I have, she

has, let me off the hook. I am no longer
a damsel, no longer listing towards quicksand
or the pull of riptides. I am *curiosity* increasingly
tuned, revving for liftoff beyond the gravity I mistook
for home. Sunlight leaks from my fingers.

LITTLE SOUL DREAMS POLARIS

Guardian of true North, lode star,
fixed point in a swirl of constellations—
it, alone, holds the same view day and night
as earth below and sky around it rotate
in a clockwork swirl of magnetic exchanges,
darkness and light passing through them
in waves—Polaris holds steady
in such surf, its eye presiding over
the Pole's vast whiteness ridged
and crevassed and mostly untouched.
Earth could well be its most articulate neighbor,
its own compass, each reflecting
in the other's view a solitude absolute,
primal and relentless: *Yes we exist—you in me,*
I in you, unpeopled white speaking to night-lit stone
over a distance no human can breach. A view
absent of any trace of others' existence
save, on some parts of the Pole, preserved
in ice and silence, a few shreds
of tattered canvas, three tins of beans
whose labels have worn away,
a kerosine lamp, and a journal
whose handwriting remains legible,
sustaining, destined to remain unread.

Little Soul Imagines the World's Second Beginning

It will receive us
like a glove that once put
pressure on warm skin
until it was peeled on and off
enough to follow every
flex of the fingers

as they grasped or let go
or tied knots among
the stems and sinews,
the roots and drying garments,
of what seems now vaguely familiar,
each acre we once claimed, never

expecting to turn away
from the gentle
approach of night, dew
gathering in the eaves,
the sun giving way to a wash
of light just before

the full moon appeared
and apples gleamed like tears
among the leaves.
Later we would just think
apples. For the taking. Not
allegorical. Not harbingers

of separations to come.

Late Bloom

takes its sweet time to accept
water. Mineral. To turn
outward to sun
that is never conditional.
The flowering
holds back until it feels
all contours of the explosion
it will become, the grit
behind the gauze, the full range
of its undiscovered shades
and blatancies.

Even in the fairest
of families, one sibling
bursts early into the world
while another holds back,
trailing doubt from ghost-roots—
hiding—until she or he grasps
that invisibility may be
a choice. Purpose
gathering.

What happened to
the high school cheerleaders
who sailed through a luminous
adolescence? To the quarterback
whose Hail Mary saved
the season, or the prom queen
living a little-girl's dream beneath
the glitter and gold of her tiara,
now nowhere to be found
on Google?

Last April one bold tree in our yard
flared pink before a late frost
seared its plumage. In July
it dropped a few stunted
apples, leavings for the deer.
The other held back
its froth, then its fruit
well past other harvests--dainty
green globes incrementally
kissed with blush, sweet
even before they ripened, but holding

to their stems and ripening more
through first snow, then
allowing themselves to be gathered
a few at a time and stored—
even as December leans
into solstice, the last
few, now slightly
withered in their bin
release, when bitten, a blinding
sweetness tinged with tart—
forthright—offering each time
the gift deeply stored.

Living with Subtraction

Choices fall away as contagion
ripples through the world, everyone
kept home, all plans on hold;
as the second half of the Selves' life
inches towards a last quarter
and expectations fade like charcoal lines
smudged by a finger tracing them
dreamily; as Little Soul and its generation
give way to *younger* and *more diverse,*
the times ripe for a change of guard,
and who's to argue? The Selves, just
beginning to feel like grown-ups, want
more time. Little Soul gazes into the fog
that has become their future, and surrenders
to a blank page. Then places
words there. Slowly
and with increasing
contentment. Pebbles along
an uncut path beneath old growth
and a sky that has always sustained
apparent emptiness.

LITTLE SOUL ON EARTH'S ESSENTIAL ALONENESS

Sometimes *I am absent,* so it seems,
but deep in this absence are stones
shaped by water that moves wherever
gravity helps it find its way around trees
and broken-off pieces of mountain.
Or in a handful of hearts carved
and polished and left at my feet
by tides. Sometimes I try to
feel, through their cracks
and pinprick caves, the Braille
of their histories, as though they could
open new maps inside me.
Nothing, not even my absence, will leave
the shape of itself when I'm gone
but I learn to take this no more to heart
than the field takes the weather,
than the sky takes clouds, than Earth
took the long solitude of its birth
into gasses and rock. All summer
it has greened beneath me and now
drops apples into my hands.

Little Soul Surrenders

Tonight, the wet earth loosens after weeks
of holding grass blades and giant cottonwoods
in place, and I have given no thought to who You
might be or whom You love best. The neighbors' gray
cat streaks across their yard with a mouse in its jaws—
I saw a small boy cradling him the other day like a large
purring sack—and I doubt I will ever give such
attention to the thought of which of Your temples
offers the best shot at an afterlife.

Now the plants release the scent of their first green,
accepting moisture from the no-longer spent soil.
The light fades. The ground weeps. The plants
breathe hard, like fish returned to their element.
Everywhere, I think, there are scraps of memory
that long to be given this rain, and a silence
that might feed them. I decant a Shiraz from the other side
of the world, pour olive oil into heated pan and select
from a string bag the season's orange and yellow offerings

while notes of a Basque accordion cascade like blown petals—
like coals sending sparks across a blackened hearth,
something to warm the amnesiac's heart—and sometimes
I believe with the largest part of my own helpless heart
that if we could let just one deep ancestral song lure us
into the abandoned sacrament of dance, we would die less
at one another's hands. There is something I've wanted
to say, tonight I can almost taste it, something surprising and right
like the rain-blessed ground that repairs itself in the dark.

LITTLE SOUL AND THE SELVES ARE ONE

Autumn in full burnish   we're flying
      down the steep hill into Valdez valley   half a mile unchecked
                  like knowing no one cares   any more   what we think
                  what we   *do*
                              so why put on the brakes?

no one
            watching if we   crash   look funky in our helmet   say what we think
                              without
                                    apology
we vanish
            into thrill   air like cold lake water
                  waking us up
                        thoughts sluicing through us
                              fresher title
                                    earlier ending
                        a sequel

benediction of cottonwoods   yellow laced with amber
                        canopy holding
                              its own light over blacktop
                                    a few fallen leaves   coins on old tar
everywhere green bleeding to gold
      don't chicken out   don't
                  use the brakes
                        mile after mile we make our own fuel
                              and accept what gravity offers
                                    now that we weigh nothing

Coda: As Wind Finds Its Way Through Walls

Your souls should have been immense by now,
not what they are,
small talking things
        —LOUISE GLÜCK

But look what they've had to overcome—
expulsion from immense privacy,
a surround of warmth and easy nurture—

as mammals, they emerged in a shock of light,
sear of oxygen, their cries inscrutable
to those eager, for a time, to receive them.

Protest, displacement, nostalgia, maybe
despair at losing a clarity they had no words for—
these fueled the helpless wailing—first

utterances—untranslatable, only understood
by parents as animal need. No wonder they
long to recover a lost language by remaking it

phrase by messy phrase, in superfluous
attempts: adolescent scribblings, therapy,
pillow talk, confession, insights seeking

drift and depth over the years as they work
their way towards reclamation beyond the single
tenuous life…. Why belittle the scraps, half-sketches,

drafts groping through flaw and foreshadowing's
of beauty?—if a soul can't speak itself incrementally
ample by such efforts, why do we struggle so, to return?

Notes

Epigraph—Excerpt from *Notes on the Soul* by Yehoshua November, *Tiferet Journal*, Spring/Summer 2021.

Little Soul and the Selves Start with the Stillness, response to lines by Louise Glück, "Faithful and Virtuous Night," from her collection, *Faithful and Virtuous Night*, Farrar, Straus and Giroux, New York, NY, 2014.

Little Soul Comes Across Lines by George Sefaris, epigraph from "The Blind Man," translated by Jennifer R. Kellogg, *The Common: A Modern Sense of Place*, July 9, 2020.

Little Soul Googles Merwin's Translation of Hadrian's Animula, *Poetry Magazine*, April 2006.

Six Lessons in Love, Section iv, *Intimacy*, epigraph from *The Hundreds* by Lauren Berlant and Kathleen Stewart, Duke University Press, Durham, NC, 2019.

Each Plant Soul Honored, quotation by Simone Weil, from *The Need for Routes*, Routledge & Kegan Paul, London, 1952.

Do-Wop Destiny, Lisa Fisher quotation taken from *Twenty Feet from Stardom*, by Morgan Neville, a documentary on backup singers of the 60's and 70's.

Little Soul Takes on T.S. Eliot, response to "Wait Without Hope…" selected lines, by T. S. Eliot, in "East Coker III," *T. S. Eliot: Collected Poems 1909-1962* (The Centenary Edition), Harcourt Brace & Company, New York, NY, 1991.

Little Soul on Earth's Essential Aloneness, after lines from Juana de Ibarbourou, *Poetry is a Heavenly Crime, Twentieth-Century Latin American Poetry*, ed. by Stephen Tapscott, University of Texas Press, Austin, TX, 1996.

Coda: As Wind Finds Its Way Through Walls, response to lines from "Retreating Wind" by Louise Glück, *The Wild Iris,* The Ecco Press, New York, NY, 1992.

Poems exploring ancestral memory were inspired by *Wounds into Wisdom: Healing Intergenerational Ancestral Trauma,* by Rabbi Tirzah Firestone, Adam Kadmon Books/ Monkfish Book Publishing Company, Rhinebeck, NY, 2019.

ACKNOWLEDGMENTS

Thanks to the following poets in our shared Poem-a-Day enterprise, when the characters Little Soul and the Selves began to surface, during the first August of the Pandemic: Sandra Blystone, Sharon Owen, Kathleen Condon, Nancy Shafer, Dale Kushner, Jean Nordhaus, Karen Kevorkian, Betsy Sholl, and Susan Aizenberg. Special thanks to Karen, Dale, and Jean—also Jody Bolz—for their feedback and encouragement on the manuscript before it found its final form, and to Betsy and Susan for their astute critiques every week on individual poems. And finally, huge thanks to my friend and editor, Andrea Watson, who vetted the manuscript too many times to count, until it found its flow and form.

I am grateful also to Ron Slate, who encouraged me early on by publishing the following poems in *On the Seawall*: "Little Soul Begins a Month of Field Notes;" "Little Soul Comes Across Lines by George Sefaris;" "Little Soul and the Selves Attempt Revision;" "Little Soul and the Selves Diverge on the Issue of Masks;" and "Little Soul and the Selves Start with the Stillness" (under the title, "Little Soul and the Selves Wander In and Out of Lines By Louise Glück").

Thanks also to Rick Jackson for publishing the suite of poems, "Six Lessons in Love," in *Poetry Miscellany*.

About The Author

Leslie Ullman is the author of six poetry collections and a hybrid collection of craft essays, writing exercises, and poems titled *Library of Small Happiness* (3: A Taos Press, 2017). A new collection based on Brian Eno's *The Oblique Strategies*, titled *Unruly Tree*, will be published in 2024 by University of New Mexico Press. Professor Emerita at University of Texas-El Paso where she taught for 27 years and established the Bilingual MFA Program, she remains a faculty member in the low-residency MFA program at Vermont College of Fine Arts. Her awards include the Yale Series of Younger Poets Award, the Iowa Poetry Prize, two NEA fellowships, and a New Mexico/Arizona Book Award for poetry. She and her husband Erik live in Taos, New Mexico.

ABOUT THE ARTIST

Dottie Moore is a studio quilt artist living in Rock Hill, South Carolina. Since 1980, her award-winning works have been exhibited, collected, and published throughout the world and commissioned by individuals, corporations, and hospitals. Her work is found in numerous galleries and has been shown in fine art/craft events, including the American Craft Council shows and The Smithsonian Craft Show. It also has been featured in publications such as *American Quilter, Art Quilt Magazine,* and *Traditional Home* by *Better Homes and Gardens*. Dottie is the founder of Piecing a Quilt of Life, an international project dedicated to empowering senior women by recognizing their creative abilities.

Of her work, she writes, "Each quilt begins with longing. The muse knocks at my door, lays cloth, paint, and thread at my feet, and then fills me with a deep longing that makes it impossible to resist the invitation to swim in the sea of possibilities once more.... I allow surprises to come. I respond, and surrender."

ALSO BY THREE: A TAOS PRESS

THE CAIRNS: NEW AND SELECTED POEMS
Bill Brown

WE ARE MEANT TO CARRY WATER
Tina Carlson, Stella Reed &
Katherine DiBella Seluja

THE UNBUTTONED EYE
Robert Carr

THE BURNINGS
Gary Worth Moody

GIRL
Veronica Golos

QUIVIRA
Karen Kevorkian

GODSPINE
Terri Muuss

ANYONE'S SON
David Meischen

VANISHES
D E Zuccone

WORLD AS SACRED BURNING HEART
Jeremy Paden

ABYSS & BRIDGE
Renée Gregorio

MANIFOLD: poetry of mathematics
E R Lutken

M
Dale M. Kushner

AGOREOGRAPHY
Jon Riccio

100 DAYS
James Navé

BLOOD SECRETS
Anita Rodriguez, Joan Ryan &
Andrea Watson

THE HEAVY OF HUMAN CLOUDS
Robert Carr